Another Story
Must Begin

Another Story Must Begin

A Lent Course Based on *Les Misérables*

JONATHAN MEYER

DARTON·LONGMAN + TODD

For Charlotte and Ellie and all who search

First published in 2013 by
Darton, Longman and Todd Ltd
1 Spencer Court
140–142 Wandsworth High Street
London SW18 4JJ

Reprinted 2014, 2018

ISBN 978-0-232-53027-8

A catalogue record for this book is available from the British Library.

Designed and produced by Judy Linard.

Printed and bound in Great Britain by Bell & Bain, Glasgow

Contents

FOREWORD   7
INTRODUCTION   9

WEEK ONE: Fantine and Cosette   21
Leaders' note   23
To start you thinking   23
SESSION ONE:
  Fantine   27
  Cosette's dream   30
  Closing prayers   32

WEEK TWO: The Bishop of Digne   33
Leaders' note   35
To start you thinking   35
SESSION TWO:
  A prayerful man formed by experience   45
  The sharing of bread and wine and an outpouring
    of grace   47
  Closing prayers   49

WEEK THREE: Jean Valjean   51
Leaders' note   53
To start you thinking   53
SESSION THREE:
  Degradation   59
  The disarming effect of grace   60
  Battles with conscience   62
  Another story must begin   63
  Closing prayers   63

WEEK FOUR: Javert   65
Leaders' note   67
To start you thinking   67
SESSION FOUR:
   Duty to the law   73
   The way of the Lord?   73
   I am the law…   74
   Closing prayers   76

WEEK FIVE: Redemption and Salvation   77
Leaders' note   79
To start you thinking   79
SESSION FIVE:
   Bring us home   85
   Who am I?   86
   Closing prayers   88

FURTHER THOUGHTS   89
END NOTES   93

Foreword

Grace Can Change Us

I often recall during my time as a valuer with one of the major auction houses visiting a client with a considerable collection to sell. He was a successful businessman, and if one were going to label him, it would be that he was of the 'Where's there's muck there's brass' school of business. He was a northerner who had got there by hard graft. He was a supporter of charitable work and gave quite a lot to the arts. It was at a time when there was considerable unrest in the country, and there was a real feeling that aspects of the structure of our society might be challenged. I said to him over lunch, 'Doesn't the breakdown of society alarm you?' I was somewhat taken aback by his response: 'No, Jonathan. I think it's absolutely marvellous, fantastic!' What so many of us fear, he saw as an opportunity.

God grant that as we walk with Christ through a broken and hurting world, we may journey on with compassion and grace, just as the Lord Jesus did, seeing our journeying as an opportunity to reach out to others in grace and love. Let us remember how powerful grace truly is to change lives, and as we experience it, exercise it, too, not knowing how it may affect the other. And let us pray that the suffering of Lent giving way to the joy of Easter may be a reality not just for us, but for all those with whom we come into contact.

Introduction

Early in March of 2012 I received a telephone call out of the blue from a location manager asking if it might be possible to consider the church of which I am priest-in-charge to be used for some filming. The church of St Mary the Virgin in Ewelme is very beautiful and has an exceptional history, so it was not uncommon to get such a request. I indicated that it would be fine for a small group to come and look over the church, although I was a little put out that they wanted to come at 7.30 the following morning. When I did open the church on that crisp morning, I was surprised to find that about twenty people arrived, and even more surprised to find the Oscar-winning director of *The King's Speech*, Tom Hooper, among them. I hadn't grasped the magnitude of the project we were being asked to help with. I had seen and knew about the stage musical version of *Les Misérables*, but I was not aware that a film was being planned.

Not much was said, but I took another call indicating that the director liked the location, and would it be possible to arrange for fake snow in the churchyard? I then began to realise that this was something a bit bigger than I had anticipated. My first responsibility was to point out that permission would be required. This process, or obtaining a faculty as it is termed, is generally dreaded by clergy, misunderstood by most and resented by churchwardens, who feel they are adequate custodians of their churches. In fact, it is a useful safeguard, especially in the case of filming, because it ensures that the nature and content to be shot is in keeping with the beliefs of the church. For example, there have been instances of satanic material for thrillers being filmed in churches, which caused considerable offence, so I was anxious to find out exactly what they wanted to film in or around the church.

I was particularly pleased to find out that the proposal was to transform the south side and porch into the exterior of the residence of the Bishop of Digne. Jean Valjean, the newly released convict, would arrive in the snow, take refuge in the porch and then be taken in by the bishop, where he would receive love and respect, food and lodging. The next day, having left early with the silver, and being brought back by the constable, the bishop exclaims, 'So there you are, I'm delighted to see you. Had you forgotten that I gave you the candlesticks as well? They're silver like the rest, and worth a good few hundred francs.'[1] Valjean is released, the gendarmes withdraw and then the bishop says to Valjean in a low voice:

Do not forget, do not ever forget, that you have promised me to use the money to make yourself an honest man. Jean Valjean my brother, you no longer belong to what is evil but to what is good. I have bought your soul to save it from black thoughts and the spirit of perdition, and I give it to God.[2]

What could be more suitable for filming in a church during Lent? The chancellor duly granted the faculty and filming took place on 21 March 2012.

On a warm, sunny day, villagers gathered by the churchyard wall to catch a glimpse of actor Hugh Jackman. There were over two hundred people involved in filming – technicians, cameramen, sound people, extras, catering staff, and numerous others. As well as the personnel, who added about 50 per cent to our normal village population, there were numerous trucks and three huge cranes supporting gigantic lights, which illuminated the scene until about 2am the next morning. By the time we arose they were mostly gone, and by the following day almost all trace of the filming had been erased. We had seen and heard Hugh Jackman, gaunt and tense (we later learned that he starved himself and went without water to achieve the effect), rushing from the church porch singing 'Another Story Must Begin'.

Only nine months later, we saw his contorted face on screen, running in anguish from the door, and our church digitised onto a rocky promontory in Provence. It was as if the transformation of our church into another place, part of a profoundly moving narrative abundant with Christian themes, could be a metaphor for how, just as Valjean is transformed by the magnanimity of the bishop, we might be transformed by Victor Hugo's majestic story.

As I was preparing for a service in late January, wondering what to do for our Lent course, I suddenly felt sure that to consider the film and reflect on the story would make an excellent basis for such a course. In scriptural terms, Lent is the forty days and forty nights that Jesus spent in the wilderness. He was led into the wilderness by the Spirit and there, during a time of prayer and temptation, he had to come to terms with his destiny. Some people will still see this period as a battle with the devil; the drama of how evil seeks to overthrow good, and how good is unshaken and prevails. Apart from the narrative of the temptations, we have no clue as to what Jesus felt or thought. But we can imagine this time of testing and of prayer as the way in which he came to terms with his humanity; the way he struggled to accept that it was his destiny to align himself with the ways of God. If fully human, he had to struggle with his conscience, as we do, and with the temptation to resist always taking the easy route. He had to become fully aware of those around him and of their needs. He had to put his ideals in line with his life and the way in which he was going to live it.

We do not approach Lent in a spirit that calls us to be Jesus, but we are called to follow Jesus. During our Lenten journey, we too should seek to try to ascertain what God's will is for us. As we will note during the chapter on the Bishop of Digne, 'Conscience is the amount of inner knowledge we possess.' To that extent, our Lenten journey should be to understand ourselves better.

By taking different characters from the story, I have tried to lead through Lent in a traditional way.

- Fantine represents our fallen state; to reflect on her life we need to contemplate sin and what that might mean in ourselves, but also in society.
- The short section devoted to Cosette seeks to counterbalance a sense of sin and our fallen nature with a hope for the future.
- The bishop marks a deeper journey of formation and the need for us to be open to the new and unexpected; we are challenged here in regards to judging others.
- Valjean and Javert represent different ways and choices; the response to our self-knowledge or, in the case of Javert, the inability to respond.
- The final section, Redemption and Salvation, tries to assess how Valjean has arrived at a sense of fulfilment and to reflect on the sacrifices he has had to make on the way; throughout, we think about the grace of God to transform lives – including our own.

But just as Hugo didn't write *Les Misérables* simply for us to enjoy a story about the deprived and dispossessed, Lent should not only be a time for reflection on our inner natures, but a time to reassess what we can do with our lives and for those around us. I hadn't expected this dimension to come through as strongly as it does, but there is real need for us to consider the state of society.

I ran a very informal course and, as we progressed, learned much about the story and how it might be used within a group to stimulate discussion, to deepen our understanding of grace (God's free, unmerited favour) and how it can alter lives. As well as the overarching theme of grace, many other strands of the story emerged. The question of punishment in contemporary society, and how much the way in which we deal with prisoners has improved (or not); moral attitudes to women and to prostitution; the dreams of youth, and how they might reflect our Christian hope of the kingdom and the restoration of our fallen nature; how we struggle with our consciences and whether we would have the strength to remain true to them, as Valjean does.

Those who enjoyed these evenings all felt that Javert was the most interesting character. He shares a difficult background with Valjean, and yet he follows what he considers a blameless career, constructing a universe upheld by cast-iron laws and unbending moral values, yet devoid of compassion. As the narrative commences with the concept of grace, it ends with that of redemption. How do we obtain redemption? Is it only Valjean, who has lived as God requires, who is redeemed? How far do the faults of Fantine's life prohibit her from entering into paradise? Was it that Javert faced eternal damnation and could not be saved, or was it that his understanding of God did not allow him to receive an outpouring of grace as Valjean did?

We are constantly aware of the secularisation of society and the marginalising of religion. There is a sense that the media does not wish to be seen to promote or entertain religious ideas, that the basics of Christian doctrine and biblical values are to be downplayed at best or ridiculed at worst. But there is much in popular culture that reflects our Christian heritage. The success of *Les Misérables* is an example of this. Hugo's themes are unmistakably Christian. During his life he was a supporter of Louis Philippe, but later became a socialist and a Roman Catholic. Although some would criticise a Christian witness that limits itself to a narrow interpretation of scriptural authority, Christian ideas and values, a Christian sense of redemption and an eschatological hope can be found in popular culture, just as they are in the film version of the musical *Les Misérables*. By looking for and reflecting on such values in secular literature and the media, we can find much that might enrich our own understanding of God, helping us to share ideas and to learn from the way others respond.

Cameron Mackintosh, who must receive the most credit for promoting the RSC version of *Les Misérables* some thirty years ago, is reported to have said that he always felt the project to be strangely blessed. In a small-group meeting during Lent in a rural and traditional benefice, I believe the themes have done more to enlighten people than past meetings.

I have sought to take the contrasting characters and use them and their place within the story to explore different themes. Of course, there will always be areas where the themes overlap and I think it a mistake to be too prescriptive about each session. I believe it is important to emphasise that *Les Misérables* does not provide definitive answers, and that different responses will not only be of value but will add a richness to the way we perceive the story. Responses to a biblical or secular text must remain open; they must pose questions for us to answer in our own way and in our own lives. Rowan Williams points out in his book *Dostoevsky: Language, Faith and Fiction* that a narrative that remains open can have a far more profound effect on us than a fable that posits all the answers:

> Whether or not we say, as earlier believers in eschatology would have done, that God is in possession of the future, the one thing we can agree on is that we are not. The open, ambiguous, unresolved narrative insists on this, which is why novels are never popular with ideologues and do not flourish in climates where eschatology is excessively realized. You do not find fundamentalist novelists (only what you would have to call fabulists, writers of narratives with closed significance).[3]

Just as the narrative remains open at least to a degree, it should point us to different possibilities and allow us to engage fully, and not, like Javert, to be constrained within a moral straightjacket.

The backdrop to the novel is the little known insurrection which took place in Paris on 6 June 1832. Since the revolution of 1789, there were several insurrections and periods of civil disturbance, as indeed there have been from time to time throughout Paris's history. The rising of 1832 was easily put down and did not cause the authorities undue concern. It gave Hugo a powerful setting for his story and a framework in which to make his case for social justice. The novel was published thirty years later, which indicates that the question of poverty was still very much on the political agenda. Any groups following the course will find it impossible not to consider how much this is still a problem in Western society or further afield. Hugo put his case forcefully within the National Assembly, and it is difficult to ignore the political aspects of the novel and the film in today's society. It is not the intention of this course to be political, but inevitably these questions may be raised. Groups might like to reflect on the role of the individual and the church as a whole to fight for social justice, and it would be a natural progression to consider Liberation Theology. The whole question of how the church responds to social injustice has been brought to the fore by both Pope Francis I and the Archbishop of Canterbury recently. Hugo alludes to the way in which people can be excluded by naming the fictional society to which the young revolutionaries Enjolras, Courfeyrac, Grantaire and others belonged as the ABC society, ABC being a play on the French word *abaissé,* abased or downcast.

As I have pointed out, there are unmistakable theological themes running through the story. One little example of the way he explicitly theologises is how he describes the response to the awful event of the Terror in Paris in 1793 and the food riots that took place at the time; that they wanted the Edenisation of the world. The ideal of returning to paradise, to our prelapsarian state and how we are redeemed is the sort of reflection ideal for a Lent course. Some of Hugo's views are very traditional, such as his approach to sin, which is evident throughout. This may encourage useful debate.

The other explicit theological theme is that of the tension between law and justice as against compassion and grace. The film is not just a confrontation between 'goodies' and 'baddies'. It explores the much more subtle and interesting question of mercy as opposed to justice, or what happens when humanity collides with the law. In modern society we are more concerned with shame than with guilt. We may not fully understand Valjean's dilemma because we are more concerned about what we can get away with, rather than what our conscience tells us is wrong.

In spite of the depressing picture of social injustice, and the way in which Fantine pays for her transgression with an early death, as well as the individual tragedies of Eponine, Gavroche and the hapless republicans, *Les Misérables* is remarkable for its profound sense of optimism. A sense of hope and belief in humanity and its future brings us back to biblical themes and to a resurrection that transcends our Lenten fast.

In order to try to exploit the full richness of *Les Misérables*, I have made use of both the recent film version and the novel. The film has telescoped parts of the novel out of necessity, but by doing so some of the subtleties have been lost. For example, there are fifty pages or so dedicated to the character of the Bishop of Digne, of which we get no sense in the film. There is a clear picture of his humility and desire to serve, in contrast to many other bishops. He eschews the trappings of his office, and we also have a picture of how his own spirituality develops; it isn't that he suddenly acts as a vessel for the outpouring of grace. There is also a fascinating encounter with an aging revolutionary responsible along with others for the death of Louis XVII, which in itself raises questions about how we are called to act. The other very important aspect of the story is the way in which Jean Valjean wrestles with his conscience when faced with the possibility of allowing the man falsely arrested in his place to be wrongfully convicted.

I would encourage readers to read the novel, but it is long. Alongside the novel, the film itself should certainly be seen. For practical purposes, either sections of the film or the soundtrack could be used during the course. I have indicated points at which to start and stop watching a section. As I have organised the course by looking at characters in order to try to emphasise a particular theme, they are not always in the same order as they occur in the film. I would urge those participating to follow the lyrics in a written version, available from www.azlyrics.com/l/lesmiserablescast. All the lyrics are very rich in biblical and spiritual allusions, and having the written text makes it easier to follow and easier to recall and reflect on the content.

We normally end our Lent courses by saying the office of Compline, which is a fitting end to the day and only takes about fifteen minutes. I generally say some short impromptu prayers, which pick up on the themes or anything particular that has come up in discussion. I have added some short suggestions for prayer at the end of each section, but of course any format or other prayers could be used.

Some useful texts to consider throughout the course

A course of this type is intended to stimulate Christian reflection on the story and its themes. The issues that emerge will be based on Christian doctrine, but most of all they will spring from biblical resonances. Many films, novels – or any work of art for that matter – can encourage us to draw such parallels and, as we have seen, *Les Misérables* is especially rich in this respect.

I would encourage people to bring their own thoughts to each session, and although I have drawn attention to some specific texts, there will be many others that occur to people and illuminate the subject in a different way. There are a few texts that I think are especially appropriate for a Lent course such as this, and which have particular resonances for *Les Misérables*. I list them below and suggest that they are read at the beginning of the course, at any time during it and again at the end. Reading them more than once will probably bring different insights to the text. There will be many others that could be added.

ISAIAH 58:1–12

A vision of hope for the future, but also an admonition about true and false worship.

The passage from Isaiah 58:1–12 is an optional Old Testament reading for Ash Wednesday. It is an excellent text to reflect on throughout Lent, which should not only be an opportunity to give things up, but to reassess how we do things. This passage comes from the end of what is often called Deutero-Isaiah, because it was written during the exile and proclaims the return of the Israelites to Jerusalem and eventually the rebuilding of the Temple. This makes it particularly symbolic for a period of Lenten reflection, because just as we await the resurrection and the triumph of Christ, we need to consider what is wrong with our lives, both personally and in the society in which we live. As we assess our past we should have a renewed vision of the future.

LUKE 10:25–37: THE PARABLE OF THE GOOD SAMARITAN

The parable of the Good Samaritan is only found in Luke's Gospel and, like all the parables, there are many layers to it. What is especially interesting in relation to *Les Misérables* is the message it has for the interpretation of the law. It is Jesus who brings the law explicitly into the discussion, but it is the way that it is understood that is important. We can imagine that both the priest and the Levite rush by not because they are inherently callous or evil; they simply have another agenda. Jesus doesn't answer the question, 'Who is my neighbour?', he turns it on its head by asking the questioner. It is not a question of finding out who we should minister to, it is a question of acting in such a way that we are perceived as a good neighbour, and making sure that our priorities are right. EZEKIEL 36:22–32

The prophet Ezekiel is perhaps the strangest of the three great Old Testament prophets. His vision comes to him during the exile, and there is considerable scholarly debate as to whether he was in Israel or in Babylon with the main body of the exiles. The distinctive character of his prophecy is that it focuses on a series of visions of what is left of the Temple in Jerusalem and how the observance of worship and the Mosaic Law had been ignored or debased. It is only by righting this that the people of Israel can return and be renewed as the people of God. One of the recurrent images is that of a heart of stone that will be renewed with a new heart.

Ezekiel was thought to be a priest himself, or certainly someone who was steeped in the traditions, practice and rituals of Temple worship. As we reflect on Jesus' own ministry, we recall his saying that he would 'destroy this temple that is made with hands, and in three days I will build another, not made with hands' (Mark 14:58). Jesus' body replaces the Temple itself. This metaphor is helpful as we consider how another story begins.

PSALM 1

The first psalm is typical of an attitude to the law which is found in several parts of the Old Testament, especially the book of Psalms itself. It represents what appears to be a rather narrow and simplistic theology. Some scholars think it may be intended to set the tone for the whole collection of Psalms. Whether this is the case or not, it gives us a message that it is only by following the tenets of the law that people will be happy or blessed and prosper in their lives. How we interpret the law will depend on how we understand such texts, but it is difficult to get away from the idea that the law is the Mosaic Law as set out in the Torah. Some parts of the Old Testament seem to challenge this approach, such as the Isaiah passage mentioned above and notably the book of Job, which recognises that those who follow the requirements of the law do not always seem to prosper.

ROMANS 3:21–26: JUSTIFICATION BY FAITH

In a sense, Paul's great theological dilemma was similar to the problem faced by Javert. Paul as a Pharisaic Jew was rooted in the belief that God had to act according to the Mosaic Law. Thus anyone who transgressed must be judged and found guilty, otherwise God could not be held to be righteous. But in and through Christ we can be made righteous by faith and by grace; thus we are justified and redeemed and God remains true to God's word. What is of fundamental importance in this passage is that salvation is open to all. It was the way sins or transgressions against the law are blotted out by grace that Javert could not understand.

WEEK ONE

Fantine and Cosette

The scribes and the Pharisees brought a woman who had been caught in adultery; and making her stand before all of them, they said to him, 'Teacher, this woman was caught in the very act of committing adultery. Now in the law Moses commanded us to stone such women. Now what do you say?' They said this to test him, so that they might have some charge to bring against him. Jesus bent down and wrote with his finger on the ground. When they kept on questioning him, he straightened up and said to them, 'Let anyone among you who is without sin be the first to throw a stone at her.'
(John 8:3–7)

Leaders' note

Introduce the course. Start the first session by making sure that everyone is familiar with *Les Misérables*. A brief informal discussion about it – and especially the characters – might be helpful before you begin. If anyone has not seen the musical or film, you can try to arrange for them to have a copy of the DVD to watch during the week. You may like to explain how the course will progress, with discussion, questions, prayer and so on. Remember, some people might be sensitive to the issues raised in this session – namely, single parenthood.

Often, in discussion, ideas may go off at a tangent, but be ready for this. It is a good idea to keep in mind roughly how long you want to spend on each session. Some guidelines are given below. Sessions work most comfortably if about an hour and a half is allowed, although these could be made shorter or longer depending on the group; you may prefer an hour, or to stretch it to two. Be aware that if you stick rigidly to the timings suggested here, you may find yourself going over or under your allotted time, so it would be best to be as flexible as possible and to check each session's content before you begin. In that way you may tailor it to suit your needs.

In this first session, the aim is to challenge your group into thinking in new ways this Lenten season.

To start you thinking

Halfway through the novel, there is a chapter entitled 'The Peep-hole'. It describes Marius contemplating whether to look through a hole in the flimsy plaster of his garret into the room next door. He finally does take a glimpse. In fact, he is looking in at the squalid quarters inhabited by the Thénadiers, although they are living under the assumed name of Jondrette. What he sees is a picture of poverty both material and spiritual. He had chosen to refuse the riches of his grandfather, but these people had no choice. And worse, these creatures were only separated from him by the flimsiest of partitions and he was unaware and uninterested in their plight. These are the eponymous people of the story, *Les Misérables*.

The passage gives us an insight into what Hugo understands by poverty. Fantine is an innocent victim. Through oppression and the weight of her responsibility for Cosette, she falls. It is the way that Fantine is overwhelmed by her predicament and falls from grace, so to speak, that gives us a valid reason why this is a good place to start.

Social justice and the imperative of making people aware of the way it dehumanises people was Hugo's passion. *Les Misérables* are those at the bottom of the pile. The dispossessed, those who struggle to earn enough to feed themselves and their families. Hugo's imagination encompasses many such characters. Ranging from Valjean the convict to the street urchin Gavroche, essentially they are victims. Some deal with their predicament and rise above it; some are raised from it by the kindness of others, such as Valjean himself; some learn to escape from poverty but lack compassion, like Javert; some profit from it, like the Thénadiers; some, such as Fantine, are engulfed by it. She encapsulates that vision of the poor being preyed upon. They are in the grip of those in power, whether it be the employer or the middleman, who wields his power perhaps even more mercilessly.

The picture of Marius living so close to such poverty divided from it by the narrowest of partitions is a powerful metaphor for how easy it is to ignore what is going on around us. Marius, although poor for the moment, has wealthy relations; he has a trained intellect, and he has benefited from an education, which enables him to earn enough to live on. The nature of poverty today may not be directly comparable with the position in the early part of the nineteenth century, but there are undoubtedly many injustices within modern

society. Putting up dividers, especially flimsy ones, is a way
of turning away from God.

Lent is a time for reflecting on how we have turned away
from God. Traditionally it is a time to consider the Fall as
represented in the book of Genesis, although we may need
to think carefully how the narrative of Adam and Eve helps
us understand the reality of our plight. In the context of
Les Misérables, it is the state of society that represents our
fall from grace. Hugo is passionate about how the French
Revolution sought to improve the lot of the oppressed.
His story underlines how poverty remained a problem as
evidenced by the insurrections of 1830 and 1832 and the
necessity for the revolution of 1848. However, he did not
give up hope. Like many nineteenth-century reformers and
thinkers, he was optimistic about the future. He believed
that *Les Misérables* really could be liberated. He wrote in
a section excluded from the novel as first published that we
should comfort and care for the masses, and educate them. He
went on to call for the opening of workshops and schools, for
the increase of wages and the decrease in working hours, and
to derive wellbeing from the social system for the benefit of
the ignorant and oppressed. He links what he calls 'fraternal
obligations' and 'political necessities'.[1]

It is not the intention for this reflection to become an
opportunity to discuss different political goals, but whatever
our politics, we should consider how we handle the poor
and the oppressed in society. What we should do is examine
our own response to the suffering that is around, regardless
of how governments attempt to deal with it. The powerful
exhortation is as more of a duty than an act of curiosity. We
need to see what these people are like and how bad things
really are, as Marius did when he decided to look through a
hole in the fragile wall.

Session One

Fantine

There is no real need to explore and explain the background to Fantine's story in any detail. It is as old as humankind. Hugo tells us simply of four young women, whom life had left with little but youth and beauty. After a summer of joy, Fantine is loved and left – left with a child, Cosette. She returns to her hometown of Montfermeil, still beautiful but with a hint of sadness in her demeanour. Here Cosette is left in the care of the monstrous Thénadiers. Fantine finds work in Montreiul in one of the factories belonging to Monsieur Madelaine (Jean Valjean), making jewellery and trinkets in jet. After losing her job, she descends into prostitution. After being wrongly accused by one of her clients and arrested by Javert, she comes to the attention of Monsieur Madelaine, the mayor, and is given support. She is ill and is placed in the factory infirmary under the care of Sister Semplice where, under the impression that the mayor will return with Cosette, the final days of her life ebb away.

Show: Watch the film from the beginning of the section entitled Montreuil 1823 until Fantine is ejected from the workshop. *(5 mins)*

Alternatively, listen to 'At the End of the Day', or read the lyrics from the sheet. *(5 mins)*

RESPONDING TO POVERTY AND THOSE IN NEED
Read: Isaiah 58:1–12 *(3 mins)*
Discuss: Take time to discuss the drudgery of the lives of

those engaged in the factory. How does this relate to the reading from Isaiah 58? *(5 mins)*

Discuss: We might consider the impact of the demands of the Isaiah passage on us personally and on our society. Do we need to respond to these demands individually or corporately? *(5 mins)*

Reflect: Both the Old and New Testaments are full of exhortations to care for the poor. Jesus reminds that we will always have the poor with us. *(2 mins)*

Read: Matthew 25:34–40 *(1 min)*

Ask: How does this passage highlight the danger of overlooking the poor in our midst altogether? *(5 mins)*

Ask: Does the line in the song about the righteous hurrying past have special resonance in the context of the Isaiah passage? *(3 mins)*

Read: Psalm 1 *(1 min)*

Reflect: In many Old Testament passages, the righteous are venerated. There are plenty of examples in the Psalms, such as Psalm 1, but there are other examples too. Can you think of any? *(3 mins)*

Discuss: Consider what and who we think of as righteous. Does Psalm 1 give us a picture of the world that we can relate to? *(3 mins)*

Read: Matthew 23:27 *(½ min)*

Reflect: Remember that in the Old and New Testaments, 'righteousness' implies adherence to the Law of Moses. What do you think of the way Jesus challenged the Pharisees in regards to their 'righteousness'? *(3 mins)*

FANTINE'S TRANSGRESSION

Reflect: Lent is a time to ponder how we have departed from God. It is traditional to think of the Fall from paradise, the sin of Adam and Eve in Eden. For any Lenten journey to have a value, we should allow ourselves to think about how we have departed from God's way personally as well as to understand what the Scriptures tell us about that departure. If we have no understanding of what we have lost, we can have little understanding of how it can be regained.

Christianity has a lot to say about sin and it often strikes me that most people don't feel especially sinful, so they feel little need for their sins to be forgiven. Just reading the story of Adam and Eve's sin and how we are tainted by that isn't particularly helpful. It may give us a vivid metaphor for the Fall, but it doesn't give us a sense of what the Fall might mean to us personally. We need to express explicitly what we mean by original sin and what it means for us as individuals.

Discuss: What do we think of when we talk of original sin? How do you think of it in terms of yourself as an individual? *(5 mins)*

Reflect: Original sin is the doctrine which rests on Augustine's interpretation; through the Fall came sin and death. The key biblical passage on which Augustine based his doctrine is Romans 5:12–21. In Western theology we inherited death and, more importantly, guilt itself. The Greek Orthodox Church interprets the Fall in a slightly different way; although death came to us through Adam's sin, we do not inherit guilt; as John Chrysostom explains, it is 'an inheritance of mortality rather than sinfulness, sinfulness merely being a consequence of mortality'.

When we come to think of Fantine, it is important for us to have some basic understanding of this if we are to ponder how her life fits into this pattern. There is little doubt that although Hugo was sympathetic to her character, he did think she was guilty and wrong in allowing herself to become pregnant in the first place. Today, some people – probably the majority – would consider her to be a victim. *(6 mins)*

Show: Watch from after the prostitution scene from 'There Was a Time When Men Were Kind' until the end of the song. *(5 mins)*

Alternatively, listen to or read the lyrics of 'I Dreamed a Dream'. *(5 mins)*

Discuss: The creation narrative in the book of Genesis tells us that we are made in the image of God (Genesis 1:26,27). Consider what this might mean to us individually, and how it is lost. *(5 mins)*

Discuss: Many questions and thoughts will spring from these lyrics, perhaps the most moving in the film. Here are few questions to think about and discuss:

Ask: What has Fantine lost? *(3 mins)*

Ask: How much is it her fault? *(3 mins)*

Ask: Can she recover her loss? *(3 mins)*

Ask: How can we, humankind, recover our own loss of righteousness? *(3 mins)*

Reflect: Think of the way Jesus dealt with 'sinners'; read 1 Corinthians 1:30. Paul's theology tries to explain that as we can never be righteous in the eyes of the law, Jesus through his life and death upon the cross becomes our righteousness *(2 mins)*

Cosette's dream

Reflect: Fantine's life has been irreparably marred. As we have seen, she has ceased to function as a human being. She has turned to stone; she has no fear, just humiliation. In the context of our Lenten course, she is the low point; she is a symbol for what has gone wrong. Of course, our lives are unlikely to have taken such a dramatic downturn, but we know that if we look through the flimsy partition that divides us from those around us, we will see many like her.

Cosette suffers, yet she is still unmarred. For modern sensibilities she is perhaps a little too perfect, but as for all the best stories, one must suspend disbelief. We can all have a vision of something that seems unattainable. After all, that is exactly what our hope should be; just as the writer of Isaiah envisions a glorious return to Jerusalem and a society where the wolf shall lie down with the lamb, so Hugo looks forward to a future where society's social problems are solved. Our Lenten journey should be about imagining our future and realigning our lives in such a way that another story can begin. *(5 mins)*

Show: Watch the very short section of the film after Valjean's escape from the infirmary and his struggle with Javert. *(2 mins)*

Alternatively, listen to or read the lyrics of 'There is a Castle on a Cloud'. *(2 mins)*

Reflect: This is an unashamedly sentimental vision. Nineteenth-century writers such as Hugo and Dickens often created a picture of a kind of idealised perfection, especially when writing about children. The church, too, adopted a very sentimental picture of the infant Jesus. That over-mawkish picture still hinders the church when it tries to emphasise a more modern theology, which presents a very human Christ, very much of the world, suffering with us; the Christ who is taunted every day in the kind of factory where Fantine works. (But in this context, the sentimentality is useful because it gives us a picture of a world that is hoped for in complete contrast to Fantine's world.) *(3 mins)*

Discuss: Take a minute or two to discuss what is attractive or not about this vision.

How does it complement or differ from your own vision of Christ? *(3 mins)*

Read: Revelation 21:1–5a, and spend some time reflecting on it. *(5 mins)*

Closing prayers

*Heavenly Father, Almighty and everlasting God, we give
    thanks for the freedom to gather freely to reflect on,
    discuss and ponder the imaginary life of Fantine.
Help us to remember that there are many Fantines around
    us today.
Help us to be aware of the difficulties facing single mothers.
Help us to understand the pressures facing young women in
    our society.*

*Grant that we may recognise that we, too, have gone astray.
Help us to understand where we have fallen short of your will.
Grant that as we seek forgiveness of sins, we may turn
    back to your ways.*

*Give us the strength to identify and bring to light social
    injustice where we find it.
Keep us from putting partitions between our own lives
    and those around us.
Give us the courage to see what lives people live and how
    bad things really are.
Keep us from daydreaming the world to rights without
    acting on our thoughts.*

*As we progress through this season of Lent, grant that we
    may see things anew and be changed.*

*We ask all this in the name of your Son, our Lord Jesus
    Christ.*

WEEK TWO

The Bishop of Digne

Surely, this commandment that I am commanding you today
is not too hard for you, nor is it too far away.
It is not in heaven, that you should say,
'Who will go up to heaven for us, and get it for us so that
we may hear it and observe it?'
Neither is it beyond the sea,
that you should say, 'Who will cross to the other side
of the sea for us,
and get it for us so that we may hear it and observe it?'
No, the word is very near to you;
it is in your mouth and in your heart for you to observe.
(Deuteronomy 30:11–14)

Leaders' note

By thinking about Fantine and Cosette, we have tried to get an insight into how the world is flawed and how that has an impact on our society and our own lives. Alongside that recognition we have allowed for the possibility of a dream in which things are put right, not just an acknowledgement that they have gone wrong. We have explored how the experiences of life formed and eventually destroyed Fantine.

This session will look at how life formed the Bishop of Digne. It is good for a Lent course to consider how we are shaped and formed by life. In the film and stage versions of the story we do not get much of an insight into the character of the Bishop of Digne, but Hugo goes to some trouble to paint a more detailed picture of him for us. On celluloid he is a figure of kindness, a figure of gentleness and, of course, it is his generosity and refusal to condemn that changes Valjean. So, here, we will look at the book as well as the filmed version of the story. Pray that your group is challenged in the area of not prejudging others, and are inspired to see how their grace-full actions can positively affect other people.

To start you thinking

In the film and stage version, we first see the bishop as he welcomes Valjean into his house. There is little for us to get a sense of what has forged his personality. But the novel goes to some lengths to give us an insight into the experiences of his life and how they added to his growth; indeed, how they led him to become the man who inspired Valjean.

Hugo is anxious to help us see that this is no ordinary bishop. He clearly had an idea of the episcopy, which accords with views of the revolutionaries of 1789, a view that is critical of the privileges of the clergy and the episcopy in particular. His first act as a bishop is to relinquish his right to live in a distinguished eighteenth-century palace with personal apartments, drawing rooms and bedrooms and a courtyard flanked by arcades in the Florentine manner, and splendid gardens. He moves into the hospital, a modest building next to the palace. This enables the palace to be used as the hospital, to house the sick in greater comfort and to take in more patients, while his modest needs are easily satisfied by the narrow two-storey house with a small garden.

Much to the annoyance of his sister, he only retains 1,000 francs of his stipend of 15,000 francs for his own personal expenses. Madame Magloire feels that he should enjoy some of the trappings of his office and at least have something of a personal income. She encourages him to apply for a carriage allowance which, after some discussion and opposition from high-minded senators, he obtains. It amounts to a further 3,000 francs. His sister at last feels they will have a little extra for comforts. However, that evening he writes a note detailing the use of the money:

Carriage and Travel Expenses

Meat broth for the hospital patients	1500 francs
Maternity Society at Aix	250 francs
Maternity Society at Draguignan	250 francs
For foundling children	500 francs
For orphan children	500 francs
	Total 3000 francs[1]

We have a picture of a saintly man who is well aware of the lives of the poor and those suffering around him. Their plight has already influenced his life and outlook.

Having established the saintly characteristics of Monseigneur Bienvenu, as he becomes known by his flock, Hugo further develops his character in a surprising way. An unusual encounter is related in a chapter entitled 'The Bishop Confronted by a Strange Light'. Digne followed a morality typical of a provincial city, conservative in its outlook; like all such communities it had an intolerance of what seemed strange or unusual. Living nearby in seclusion was a former revolutionary, who although not directly responsible for his death had brought the former King Louis XVI to trial. He was also an atheist, banished and excluded, living alone in a primitive dwelling in an isolated valley.

In spite of the bishop's generosity, kindness and self-sacrifice, he almost unconsciously harbours some prejudice. For some time he felt he should visit this individual and yet, without him realising it, the former revolutionary inspired a repugnance in him, which could even be described as hatred. In such a way it caused a sense of estrangement. The bishop's instincts are that as shepherd he should not avoid a 'sick' sheep and yet, at the same time, he sets out to make the visit and turns back several times. On hearing that the elderly outcast is ill, he finally makes the journey. When he meets the dying man, the bishop feels uncomfortable enough not to shake his hand. The bishop asks him of his past and it is clearly his intention to reprimand him and to bring him to an understanding of what the bishop would describe as past sins.

Like most of us, the bishop approaches the encounter with preconceptions; he believes he has an understanding of the way in which this man has gone astray, and although he seeks to reach out to him, he reaches out on his own terms. During this initial conversation the man, who is referred to as Monsieur G, says:

Man is ruled by a tyrant whose name is Ignorance, and that is the tyrant I sought to overthrow. That is the tyrant which gave birth to monarchy, and monarchy is authority based on falsehood, whereas knowledge is authority based on truth. Man should be ruled by knowledge.'

'And by conscience,' said the bishop.

'They are the same thing. Conscience is the amount of inner knowledge that we possess.'[2]

They talk of the French revolution, of the downfall of the king, of what was good about the revolution. The bishop remains unconvinced and asks about the Reign of Terror, that period of anarchy and chaos which tore France apart. He abhors the use of violence and instinctively supports the monarchy, without considering what that meant for society in late eighteenth-century France. Here the revolutionary seems on weaker ground, but the discussion then hinges on the death of the young Louis XVII, who died in prison at the age of 10 on 8 June 1795 in Paris.

'Louis XVII. What are you mourning? An innocent child? If so, I will weep with you. But if you are mourning a royal child I will ask you to consider. To me the case of the brother of Cartouche,[3] an innocent child who was hanged by the armpits on the Place de Grève until he died, for no other crime than that he was the brother of Cartouche, is no less grievous than that of the grandson of Louis XV, an innocent child martyred in the Temple for the crime of being the grandson of Louis XV.'

'I do not care for that association of names,' said the bishop.

'Cartouche? Louis XV? To which do you object?'

There was a brief silence. The bishop was almost sorry he had come; yet he felt obscurely and strangely moved.

'Monsieur Le Pretre,' said the dying man, 'you do not care for the cruder aspects of truth. Christ cared. He drove the money-lenders from the Temple. His scourge was a great teller of truths. When he said, "Suffer them to come unto me", he made no distinction between the children. He would have made no bones about associating the son of Barabbas with the son of Herod. Innocence wears its own crown, Monsieur; it needs no added dignity; it is as sublime in rags as in royal robes.'[4]

The bishop is moved by this exchange. There follows a dialogue in which the revolutionary goes on to ask the bishop

why he should question him and ask him about the terrible
years of the revolution. He is a prince of the church, a man of
wealth and influence, and a man who commands respect, well
provided for with a substantial palace and staff. No doubt his
carriage is waiting out of sight in the trees. The revolutionary
wants to know where his true authority comes from. The
bishop doesn't disabuse him with regard to the way in which
he lives his life, but accepts his criticism, even though it is
unfounded but asks how this all proved that compassion was
not a virtue, and clemency a duty, and that 1793 was not
unforgivable.

The discussion hinges on the rights and wrongs of the
French revolution. The obvious truth was that many wrongs
of the *ancien regime* deserved to be righted. The equal truth
that atrocities were committed on each side, the conclusion
of the dying man, gives us a view of the tragedies of human
suffering. He believes that humanity has advanced through
struggles and revolutions. Even though he is considered
an atheist, he states that progress must believe in God.
Presumably he is thought of as an atheist because he does
not support the church in the state in which he found it. As he
dies, he thinks of God as the infinite. The bishop is profoundly
moved and suggests that the moment is offered to God. The
response of the dying revolutionary is worth reading in full.

'I have passed my life in meditation, study, and
contemplation. I was sixty when my country summoned
me to take part in her affairs. I obeyed the summons. There
were abuses and I fought against them, tyrannies and I
destroyed them, rights and principles and I asserted them.
Our country was invaded and I defended it; France was
threatened and I offered her my life. I was never rich; now
I am poor. I was among the masters of the State, and the
Treasury vaults were so filled with wealth that we had to
buttress the walls lest they collapse under the weight of
gold and silver; but I dined in Poverty Street at twenty-two
sous a head. I succoured the oppressed and consoled the

suffering. I tore up the altar-cloths, it is true; but it was to bind our country's wounds. I have always striven for the advance of mankind towards the light, and sometimes I have resisted progress that was without mercy. I have done my duty, and what good I could, so far as was in my power. And I have been hounded and persecuted, mocked and defamed, cursed and proscribed. I have long known that many people believe they have the right to despise me, and that for the ignorant crowd I wear the face of the damned. I have accepted the isolation of hatred, hating no one. Now at the age of eighty-six I am on the point of death. What do you ask of me?'

'Your blessing,' said the bishop, and fell on his knees.

When at length the bishop raised his head there was a look of grandeur on the old man's face. He had died.[5]

The bishop went to minister to a dying man with the expectation that he would offer him a blessing and absolution, but it is he who seeks a blessing. It is this unexpected encounter that changes the bishop most profoundly. He is naturally a man of compassion, a man who followed the teaching of Jesus, a man who lived modestly, but this encounter adds a complexity and depth to his faith.

It is never simple to decide what is right or wrong; there is always a complexity to reaching a morally defensible position. It is a mistake to regard issues as being always clear-cut. We have a tendency to read history as if it was like a Hollywood western with 'goodies' and 'baddies' lined up against each other. We know that many conflicts raging around the world are wrong, but we must recognise that good people are caught up in them.

In the church at Ewelme there is a wall monument to a General Francis Martyn. During the English Civil War he was a commander in Cromwell's army, and although little is known of his life, he must have come from a good family. It is reported that after the battle of Chalgrove, when royalist forces were defeated, he made sure that the doors of the church in

Ewelme were locked to prevent the victorious Puritan troops from destroying some of the very fine monuments inside, which included the late fifteenth-century alabaster tomb of Alice de la Pole, Duchess of Suffolk and grand-daughter of Geoffrey Chaucer. The tomb is well preserved to this day.

There is a lesson here for those of us brought up to think of Roundheads and Cavaliers as utterly opposed to each other and distinct in their views. Francis Martyn must have been opposed to King Charles I and have harboured republican views, and yet in matters of theology he may well have followed the Laudian party. He was clearly unsympathetic to extreme Puritan views about the use of images and statuary in churches. More recently and disastrously, modern conflicts between Islamic and Fundamentalist Christian ideologies have been presented in similarly black and white terms.

There is a subtle message for the church and the clergy here. The bishop is undoubtedly a good and worthy individual, yet there is a hint of arrogance in his approach to this man. He makes assumptions about right and wrong and about the motives of his parishioner. As Keith Jones reminds us, 'the first duty of the follower of Jesus is to point to the wild grace that we find in the world around us; the people who put us to shame by their immediate response to the people next to them, ourselves included.'[6]

The parable of the Good Samaritan is a warning to the organised church. It is not so much that the priest and the Levite deliberately pass by on the other side, it is that they have another agenda. They are about the business of the Temple and they fail to see beyond their immediate flock. Clergy are often tempted to restrict themselves to the congregation. This is the message the bishop takes from this encounter.

He returns home and remains in thought and deep prayerfulness for some time. Around him he encounters prejudice. Why did he make a visit to such an old scoundrel? Surely he did not secure a deathbed conversion, so he must have gone to witness a soul being carried off by the devil. But thereafter his tenderness and solicitude for the defenceless and afflicted is doubled; he seeks to alleviate suffering whenever he encounters it. He sees that the overriding commandment is to love one another, and only by doing so can the soul truly expose itself.

It is through this outpouring of love that Valjean is transformed. Valjean is his success. The mayor reads in the paper that the bishop has died some years later, and he wears mourning clothes. He has had no contact or knowledge of him, and no doubt the bishop has no knowledge of the man he assisted.

We can never know how little acts of kindness and compassion will play out in the world.

Like all of us, the bishop is formed by experience. The many courses designed to train clergy will have an element which loosely comes under a similar heading: formation. Formation is not intended to be something that can be learned or can be arrived at in simple easy stages. At best, it is a process that continues over a lifetime. In the context of a course, it is often associated with a period of having one's own beliefs (or prejudices) being undermined and confronted so that when they are challenged in practice it is easier to rise to that challenge. In some cases, views will change. I remember hearing Rabbi Lionel Blue relating how as a young man he underwent psychoanalysis following a period of mental stress. He asked the therapist if through such analysis he would lose his faith. The answer came that he would lose it only if it was a function of neurosis. Whether we are training for the priesthood or not, we are all formed by our experiences; we should remember that we all have a ministry that is shaped by them, and should channel our gifts:

> We have gifts that differ according to the grace given to us: prophecy, in proportion to faith; ministry, in ministering; the teacher, in teaching; the exhorter, in exhortation; the giver, in generosity; the leader, in diligence; the compassionate, in cheerfulness.

> Romans 12:6–8

The idea of the church can be like a straightjacket; it can restrict us, and it is probably for this reason that Hugo himself moved away from the centralising structures of the Roman Catholic Church. For those of us who feel that the 'church' does not always offer us the sustenance we need, it is worth remembering the etymology of the word. In the Greek it is simply *ecclesia,* a gathering; a distinction that caused tension for those who first translated the Bible into English and highlighted by David Edgar in his play, *Written on the Heart.* The church does not need to have a narrow definition and, indeed, it is how we live our lives outside church that is important. How we reflect on the experiences of our own lives is important not just to us but to those around us. Just as the bishop could have no idea of how his life affected Jean Valjean, we can have no idea of how the littlest of things can influence and encourage people in ways we will never know.

Session Two

A prayerful man formed by experience

Reflect: Without the bishop there would be no story. It is his act of kindness and mercy that sows a seed in the heart of Valjean. From that seed, lives are changed. For that reason it is worth considering what kind of man he was and, in the context of the novel, how he was formed. Take a few moments to reflect on and consider how the bishop lived his life. *(5 mins)*

Ask: What was most important to him? *(2 mins)*

Read: Luke 10:25–37 *(2 mins)*

Discuss: Does the parable of the Good Samaritan inform our understanding of the church, and our duty as Christians? *(5 mins)*

Ask and discuss: The bishop is reluctant to see his parishioner and turns back several times.

Have we experience of avoiding tasks we know we should undertake?

When we finally get round to tackling difficult issues, how do we feel afterwards?

How far was the bishop open to new ideas and ways of looking at things?

Did he realise that he had prejudged the revolutionary recluse?

Did he tend to see things in black and white?

How far do we have fixed views?
How far do those around us have fixed views? *(10 mins)*

Read:

Do not judge, and you will not be judged; do not condemn,
and you will not be condemned. Forgive, and you will be
forgiven; give, and it will be given to you. A good measure,
pressed down, shaken together, running over, will be put
into your lap; for the measure you give will be the measure
you get back. (Luke 6:37,38) *(1 min)*

Ask: Does the bishop make a judgement on Monsieur G?
(2 mins)

Discuss: The bishop is accused of avoiding the cruder aspects
of truth. Is this fair? *(2 mins)*

Reflect: As we reflect on the old man's death, we can see
that he believed that he had lived life as well as he could,
although he had not supported the traditional structures of the
church. Jesus died without supporting many of the traditional
structures of Judaism at the time. Like the old man, he cared
about social justice, as Isaiah did, and in that sense his death
was a critique of Jewish preconceptions. *(3 mins)*

Ask: Does this old man's death help us to make a constructive
critique of some Christian preconceptions? *(3 mins)*

Discuss: Is it fair to say that the bishop realised that the old
man had tried to make the world a better place, but that he had
faced very difficult choices in the process? *(2 mins)*

Reflect: 'Conscience is the amount of inner knowledge
we possess.' These words of Monsieur G are a perceptive
comment on how we view ourselves. It is so easy to overlook
aspects of our characters, just as the bishop assumes he has
the moral high ground when he visits the recluse. The bishop

has made the mistake of imagining that Monsieur G should have lived life according to his rules, and of failing to see that he lived life in the way that he thought best under the circumstances. *(3 mins)*

Reflect: God sees the heart (see 1 Samuel 16:7). How far do we find ourselves judging others, when we do not know their heart motivations or what had led them into their situation, or to act in a certain way? Spend a few moments thinking about your own attitudes, and bringing them before God. *(2 mins)*

Discuss: How open are we to begin to see things from a new, unexpected and different point of view, so that we might exercise more compassion? *(3 mins)*

The sharing of bread and wine and an outpouring of grace

Reflect: We have a picture of an extraordinary man. A man who lives life simply and has a simple understanding of the gospel. He is the kind of man we do not often meet. *(2 mins)*

Show: Watch the scene where Valjean is taken to the mayor's office, then arrives by night at the bishop's house and is taken in until he steals out into the night. *(2 mins)*

Read: Luke 24:28–31 *(1 min)*

Reflect: For Christians, there is obvious symbolism in the bishop's offering of bread and wine. But they are potent symbols of hospitality and friendship for all. For Valjean, arriving tired, hungry and dispossessed, they represent physical sustenance and have no spiritual significance. For Cleopas and his friend in the passage we have read, they also represent sustenance after a long trek until their eyes are opened. And, they have just witnessed the extraordinary events in Jerusalem, and knew something of the life and death of Jesus.

Valjean did not have such thoughts uppermost in his mind. We may assume that all had a good knowledge of Christianity and underwent a basic Christian education, but in nineteenth-century Europe many of the poor would have had no such instruction. Many of us make the same assumptions today. The truth is that in countless parts of society, there is almost a complete lacuna of understanding. It was not through teaching that the bishop could communicate his message, but through an act of love. *(2 mins)*

Show: Watch the remainder of the scene, when Valjean is brought back by the constables until the bishop blesses him. *(2 mins)*

Alternatively, listen to or read the lyrics of 'The Bishop', noting especially the bishop's words to Valjean. The words that do start another story. *(2 mins)*

Discuss: Reflect on and discuss the bishop's words, thinking about what is meant by:

1. Leaving the best behind;
2. A higher plan;
3. The witness of martyrs;
4. The passion, the blood. *(10 mins)*

Reflect: What has come into being 'in him was life, and the life was the light of all people. The light shines in the darkness, and the darkness did not overcome it' (John 1:4,5). *(2 mins)*

Discuss: End by thinking and sharing about what it means to be raised out of darkness. In what ways might we be called to bring the gospel to those who have no basic knowledge of Christianity today? *(10 mins)*

Closing prayers

*Heavenly Father, Almighty and everlasting God, we thank
    you for all the gifts and encounters of this day.*
*Help us to have the wisdom to reach out to those around us
    and not to prejudge them.*
*Help us to understand that however we live our lives, they
    can be enriched further by other people. Help us to have
    the wisdom to acknowledge that we are all faced by
    difficult moral choices.*

O Lord, grant that we may continue to learn and change.
O Lord, grant that our lives may help and enlighten others.
*O Lord, grant that we may remember that our deeds may
    change or inspire others in ways we could never have
    dreamed of.*

WEEK THREE

Jean Valjean

I will give them one heart, and put a new spirit within them;
I will remove the heart of stone from their flesh
and give them a heart of flesh,
so that they may follow my statutes and keep my
ordinances and obey them.
Then they shall be my people, and I will be their God.
(Ezekiel 11:19, 20)

Leaders' note

In this session, we look at Jean Valjean. Valjean is the main character of *Les Misérables*. It is his life and deeds that are central to the story. Through his life he influences and changes others. But it is the way in which he is changed and transformed that is the key to the narrative. The aim here is to get your group thinking about transformation; that the freely given forgiveness and grace of God really can transform a life. We can receive this grace for ourselves, and we should extend that grace to others.

To start you thinking

We have considered the character of the Bishop of Digne; how he behaves uncharacteristically for a bishop at that time (and probably at any time), and how his simple and faithful way of life following the precepts of the gospel had such an impact on Valjean. We have also reflected on how the bishop himself changed and adjusted the way he lived as a response to faith and to what he saw in others. By considering and reflecting on Valjean's response to the extraordinary trust and munificence of the bishop, we can gain insights into how we respond to grace, and how our actions could change and influence others. During Lent when I first ran this course shortly after the release of the film, a traveller or wanderer was found sleeping in the south porch of our church, exactly where the imaginary Valjean had laid his head outside the Bishop of Digne's palace. He was discovered early on a very cold Sunday morning before our 8.00am service of Holy Communion. One of the congregation gave him something to eat, but by the time the service was over he had left.

It is easy to forget that although we are dealing with a work of fiction, the events imagined and described would have been commonplace in the nineteenth century. We can easily blind ourselves to thinking that they may not be so commonplace today.

It doesn't take much to imagine people still living in despair as Fantine did, and there are still plenty of people sleeping rough. There are also young men and women emerging from prison with no plans for their future and little support. I spent a short time during training for ordination on placement in a young offender institution. One day I asked the chaplain how many of the 'boys' (some of them were only 15) did not re-offend, and what effect prison had on them. He answered that around 10 per cent wanted to reform themselves and had the education and family support to do so, that around 45 per cent wanted to reform themselves but lacked any support outside prison and found it very hard to do, and that the remaining 45 per cent had made a career choice.[1] This imposes a burden on all of us to consider not only how such people can be valued, but also how they can be materially helped so as to enable themselves to be free from the lure of crime.

In the story, the traveller is received. He is also surprised by the reception he gets, as it is so different from elsewhere. Valjean has been turned away from inns and other places where he might obtain sustenance and refuge since leaving Toulon, four days before, walking about thirty miles a day. Even the prison guard wouldn't let him in. He knocks on the bishop's door not knowing whose dwelling it might be. Of course, it isn't the official bishop's palace as that has been given up to the hospital. At last he is taken in.

Valjean enjoys the hospitality of the bishop, whom he mistakes for a curate. After a good night's sleep and food, he steals out of the house early, taking the silver. He knows that he will soon be apprehended. It is as if he is unable to shake off the label society has attached to him.

When he is caught and returned, his world is turned upside down. He expects to endure another nineteen years imprisoned and yet the bishop beams at him that he is delighted to see him in case he had forgotten to take the candlesticks he had given him as well. It is now that we can consider the effect the bishop had on Valjean. It is only through the unexpected act of kindness that he begins to look inwards, and to examine himself. As he departs, he realises his mindset has been challenged.

> When he left the bishop's dwelling Jean Valjean … had been in a state of mind unlike anything he had ever experienced before and was quite unable to account for what was taking place within him. He had sought to harden his heart against the old man's saintly act and moving words. 'You have promised me to become an honest man. I am buying your soul. I am rescuing it from the spirit of perversity and giving it to God.' The words constantly returned to him and he sought to suppress them with arrogance, which in all of us is the stronghold of evil. Obscurely he perceived that the priest's forgiveness was the most formidable assault he had ever sustained; that if he resisted it his heart would be hardened once and for all, and that if he yielded he must renounce the hatred which the acts of men had implanted in him during so many years, and to which he clung. He saw dimly that this time he must either conquer or be conquered, and that the battle was now joined, a momentous and decisive battle between the evil in himself and the goodness in that other man.[2]

We should be mindful that there is a distinction between the forgiveness offered to Valjean, and the silver, which gives him a practical advantage in life. While we can feel free from sin through grace, many disadvantaged still struggle in life and require both practical and spiritual support. However, it is worth contemplating whether the two can be separated. If we think back to the passage from Isaiah, they are interdependent. It is of no use praying for the poor – or for anything at all, for that matter – if we are not prepared to try to do something about it, however little.

As the story of *Les Misérables* progresses, it introduces us to a man apparently unconnected with Jean Valjean. Père Madelaine, a manufacturer of jet, or 'black glass', in the town of Montreuil-sur-Mer, through a simple improvement in the material used for the manufacture, began to build a very successful business. He soon became immensely rich and popular and was twice nominated as mayor for the town, but refused. Being asked a third time, he eventually accepted. It was said that the angry words of an old woman shouting from a doorway had most effect on him: 'A good mayor is a useful person. How can you hold back when you have the chance to do good?'[3]

Valjean's old adversary, Javert, becomes chief of police in the town and regards Père Madelaine with suspicion. When Madelaine uses his immense strength to rescue a man trapped by a broken cart, Javert believes that he has at last found Jean Valjean, known for his unusual strength, but he has no proof. Later, when Javert writes to the authorities in Paris, he is told that he cannot have found Valjean, as he is in custody in Arras. Of course, Père Madelaine is Jean Valjean. It is when Javert relates this to the mayor that Valjean is faced with a terrible moral dilemma. Only he and the man being held in Arras (Champmathieu) know that they have the wrong man. In admitting his mistake and asking to be relieved of his duties, Javert has inadvertently sown the seed for a gargantuan moral struggle.

Jean Valjean has been formed by the accidents of his life and by the initial act of grace in the magnanimity of the Bishop of Digne. But he changes and develops slowly and steadily. Here he is faced with the simple choice of continuing to enjoy his success in the knowledge that an innocent man has been mistaken for him, or revealing himself and losing all his worldly wealth, comfort and influence. The psychological drama of his dilemma is absolutely central to the way in which he grows, to his overriding compassion and to his eventual redemption.

The struggle Valjean faces with his own conscience is surely familiar to most of us. I remember as quite a small boy thinking what a nuisance a conscience can be. One afternoon, finding myself alone in the changing rooms at school, I noticed that another pupil had left a few pounds in his pocket. Even one pound would have been worth taking in the early seventies. I thought to myself how much easier life would be if one had no conscience. At university, I had a friend who, like most of us, found the necessity to get down to study rather difficult. Across the corridor he had a colleague who never seemed to stop working and he was referred to as my friend's 'conscience'. Conscience sometimes seems inconvenient, and even when we feel at peace with the world it can intrude – how we wrestle with what makes us uneasy, how we deal with difficulties in the workplace that are not our own responsibility, how we rationalise our own omissions. The power of Valjean's struggle with himself does not come across so strongly in the film. In the book, he agonises over whether to give himself up or not:

'After all,' he thought, 'what am I afraid of? Why do I have to sit here brooding? I'm safe at last. The one door through which the past might have entered to disrupt my life has now been closed, walled-up for good. The man who so nearly guessed the truth who did guess it, by God! – Javert, the bloodhound sniffing at my heels, has been thrown completely off the scent. He has got his Jean Valjean and will trouble me no more. Very likely he will choose to leave the town and go elsewhere. And none of this is my doing. I had no part in it. So what is wrong? To look at me one might think that I had been overtaken by disaster. But after all, if another man is in trouble, that is not my fault. Providence has ordained it, and who am I to fly in the face of Providence? What more can I ask? The blessing I have most longed for; during these years, the subject of my nightly dreams and prayers to Heaven, has now been granted me – perfect security! God has caused it to happen, and it is not for me to oppose the will of God. And why does God want it? So that I may continue as I have begun, to do good in the world and to set an example to other men, to let it be seen that the way of virtue and repentance is not divorced from happiness. I no longer understand why I was afraid to visit the curé, confess to him and ask his counsel, when clearly that is what he would have said to me – the matter has been settled, leave things as they are, let God have His way.'[4]

But he is drawn back to what is right. He cannot let an innocent man be punished. His agony is prolonged as he has trouble finding a vehicle to get him to Arras; it breaks down on the way. Surely, he thinks, this is God's way of letting him know that he can be free, that he can allow an innocent man to be condemned; after all, it happens all the time. He reaches the court just in time – just before the case is ended and the hapless Champmathieu is condemned. The dilemma for Valjean is summed up in his words, 'If I speak I am condemned, if I stay silent I am damned.' As he surrenders himself he blurts out these words to the judge:

You are right in supposing that Jean Valjean was a very evil wretch, although perhaps the fault was not wholly his. It is not for a man so lowly to remonstrate with Divine Providence or seek to advise society, but the degradation from which I sought to escape is none the less an evil thing. It is gaol that makes the gaolbird, and this is something that you must bear in mind. Before going to prison I was a peasant with very little intelligence, almost an idiot. It was prison that changed me. I had been stupid but I grew malignant, like a smouldering log that bursts into flame. Goodness and compassion saved me after brutality had come near to destroying me. But these are things that I cannot expect you to understand.[5]

Although there is much more to the story of Valjean, we will leave his confrontation with Javert, his discovery of the power of love through his relationship with Cosette, and his encounter with Marius to the next two sessions.

Session Three

Degradation

Show: Watch from the beginning of the film until Jean Valjean leaves the boatyard. *(5 mins)*

Alternatively, listen to the opening number, 'Look Down', or read the lyrics. *(2½ mins)*

Read: The command to 'look down' gives us a powerful image of submission. Isaiah uses it to portray the suffering and humiliation of the exiles in Babylon:

> 'See, I have taken from your hand the cup of staggering:
> you shall drink no more
> from the bowl of my wrath.
> And I will put it into the hand of your tormentors,
> Who have said to you,
> 'Bow down that we may walk on you';
> and you have made your back like the ground
> and like the street for them to walk on.'
>
> (Isaiah 51:22,23) *(1 min)*

Discuss: Consider what it means to look down. How does this affect the way we value ourselves and how we are valued by others? How does Valjean see himself? Has his sentence changed him? How has the civil law dealt with him? *(5 mins)*

Reflect: In the Acts of the Apostles, we hear how Paul is cast down by the power of God on the road to Damascus.

Although the circumstances are different, the image of being cast down and then commanded to get up and stand upon one's feet to testify to the power of God resonates with the picture of subjection. *(3 mins)*

Read: Acts 26:12–18 *(1 min)*

The disarming effect of grace

The most significant moment in the story comes as the Bishop of Digne tells the gendarme who captured Valjean with the stolen silver that he had given the silver to the ex-convict. We have thought about how the act of grace is transforming and how the bishop's experience of life led him to act in such a way. But it is the effect this act of compassion has upon Valjean that is central to the story. He is perplexed and confused and cannot get it out of his head.

Watch the film from the beginning of Valjean's soliloquy, 'What Have I Done, Sweet Jesus?' until he emerges from the church. *(3½ mins)*
  Alternatively, listen to or read the lyrics of 'Valjean's Soliloquy'. *(3½ mins)*

Read: Matthew 5:38–46 *(1 min)*

Ask: How is Valjean's world challenged? *(3 mins)*

Ask: What has he known up to this point in life? *(3 mins)*

Reflect: The novel brings out the psychological drama which faces Valjean more explicitly.

He had sought to harden his heart against the old man's saintly act and moving words. 'You have promised me to become an honest man. I am buying your soul. I am rescuing it from the spirit of perversity and giving it to God.'⁶ *(2 mins)*

Read: The act of kindness is almost destructive in the way that it disturbs him. The message of the prophets frequently tells of the refusal and apparent inability of the people to listen to the Word of God. Ezekiel, Jeremiah and Isaiah often return to this theme. Here are a few relevant verses:

Ezekiel 3:7
Ezekiel 11:19, 20
Ezekiel 18:31, 32
Jeremiah 24:7
Isaiah 43:19 *(5 mins)*

Ask: Do we 'harden our hearts'? *(3 mins)*

Reflect: Do we need to ask God to soften our hearts? *(2 mins)*

Ask: Do we recognise the way in which Valjean feels assaulted by grace? *(3 mins)*

Read: John 13:31–35 *(1 min)*

Discuss: It is unusual to be commanded to love someone. How can we respond to such a command? *(3 mins)*

Discuss: This has parallels in the way the bishop tells Valjean he must use this silver to become an honest man. How does Valjean respond to the bishop's exhortation, and is this a sudden transformation? *(5 mins)*

Ask: Are we compelled to respond to an outpouring of grace? *(3 mins)*

Ask: Is it the gift of silver that begins to transform Valjean, or is it the fact that he is forgiven? *(3 mins)*

Battles with conscience

Reflect: Although Valjean has resolved that another story must begin, he is still troubled by conscience, as we have seen by the inner turmoil he experiences when he has the chance to allow an innocent man to be wrongly identified as him. Most of us, naturally, simply do not possess the courage displayed by Valjean to give himself up. *(2 mins)*

Show: Watch the section of the film from when Javert receives the letter from Paris informing him that Valjean is being held in Arras and that his suspicions must be wrong, until Valjean confesses in the courtroom, 'Who am I? 24601.' *(4 mins)*

Read: John's account of Peter's denial, John 18:15–18, 25–27 *(1 min)*

Discuss: When we are faced with hard decisions which will cause us some kind of discomfort, we are often tempted to take the easy route. Think about a time when your conscience has really troubled you. Did you ignore it? Or not? What were the consequences? Did you grow through the experience? *(5 mins)*

Reflect: The key elements in Valjean's life are his petty theft of bread, which leads to conviction, a long imprisonment and a loss of his own self-value and identity, his encounter with the Bishop of Digne and his response to the bishop's act of mercy. Although by the time he becomes mayor he has already changed, he still faces other challenges and continues to develop. Likewise, we too continue to grow and develop through life's challenges and trials. Think of some of the choices you have made recently. What do those choices tell you about yourself, your faith, and your own heart's motivation? *(3 mins)*

Another story must begin

Reflect and discuss: We have touched on visions of the future in Isaiah 58:1–12, in Revelation 21:1–5a and in the imaginings of Cosette. Valjean reflects that if there was another way to go, he had missed it twenty years before.

Did he have an option?

Do we remember times when we might have taken another path? What stopped us? What might 'another story' be? *(5 mins)*

Show: Watch the section from Cosette and Valjean's departure from the Thénadiers until their arrival at the north gate in Paris. *(3 mins)*

Alternatively, listen to or read the lyrics of 'Suddenly'. *(2½ mins)*

Read: John 21:15–19 *(1 min)*

Reflect: Jesus reinstated Peter; God's grace is available to reinstate us when we fail, too. Just as Valjean was changed through his experience with the bishop, God's transforming love and grace will affect our lives and decisions and can truly make us different people, effective for God. *(3 mins)*

Closing prayers

Heavenly Father, Almighty and everlasting God, we thank you for the gift of music and song, for the creative imaginations of those around us; as we reflect on and talk about Les Misérables, *help our hearts to be moved by what we find.*

We pray for those forced by circumstance to look down; help lift their eyes to the stars.

*We pray for the gift of grace, that we may understand the
   generosity of sacrifice.*

*Help us to choose the right path and turn back from our
   wrong turnings.*

*Deliver us from temptations, but when we are faced with
   moral dilemmas, help us to act with strength and integrity.*

WEEK FOUR

Javert

So you also, when you have done all that is
commanded you, say, 'We are unworthy servants;
we have only done what was our *duty*.'
(Luke 17:10, RSV, my italics)

Leaders' note

In this session we are dealing with Javert, his conflicting thoughts and attitudes and his ultimate demise. Be aware that because this session will touch on suicide, there might be some people in the group who may be strongly affected.

Although we have seen the effect of grace upon Valjean, and the changed life that ensues, when faced with grace, Javert reacts differently. In this session, we will confront the powerful emotions that come when a world-view is challenged. Aim to help people to think deeply about the issues raised. It may throw up many questions for the individual. How will we respond when presented with an extravagant grace and forgiveness we don't deserve? Do we think God's grace is for all, or are some exempt? Is it for others, not for us? Is this course even challenging our view of the nature and character of God?

To start you thinking

Javert is one of the great creations of fiction. It is often said that the devil gets the best tunes. Likewise, some of the best characters in fiction are the 'bad' ones. There is something that draws us to such characters. There is a fascination in what makes them tick. In one of the rather long historical sections of the book, Hugo refers to the Catholic bishop Jacques-Bénigne Lignel Bossuet, a well-known opponent of Protestantism who is reputed to have continued to sing the *Te Deum* as Protestants were being massacred. I am reminded of the chief of police, Scarpia, in Puccini's opera *Tosca*, who also sings the *Te Deum* while he dreams of possessing Tosca. Javert shares the self-belief of these characters; he sees no need to question things or to question himself. But it would be simplistic to think of him as a typical villain. In fact, what makes him really interesting is that he is not really a villain at all. He simply has a narrow view of the law, and what today we would think of as a distorted sense of justice. He tries to enforce the law as it is without questioning it. Indeed, to him the very idea of questioning it at all would be wrong.

He was born in prison, his mother was a fortune-teller and his father had served a sentence on the galleys, like Valjean. He always felt himself to be an outsider. For him society was divided between those who maintained its structures and those who preyed on it. He did well in the police. For him authority was paramount; he honoured it to the extent of idolatry, and anything that challenged it was evil. For him the law could not be wrong. He lived a life of unswerving duty.

He is the cruel police officer responsible for subjugating and eventually releasing Valjean on parole; he is also the officer answerable to Valjean as the Mayor of Montreuil. To his credit he shows great shame when he believes he has wrongly suspected the mayor of being Valjean, and asks to be dismissed; such is his dedication to duty and his sense of the order of things. But when he realises that he was correct, he shows no mercy.

He is obsessed by catching Valjean simply because he broke parole and stole a coin after his release from the galleys. The way in which Valjean's life has changed, in which he supports the poor and encourages wealth cannot take away the stain of his crime. Javert reveals that he has had a similar background to his adversary, but he has escaped from it and consequently he despises those who have not. But as he gets close to his goal, his world begins to fall apart.

There is a touching moment in the film when Javert, surveying the dead comrades laid out after their slaughter on the barricades, comes to the body of the street urchin Gavroche. He calmly removes his own medal and places it on the boy's corpse as a sign of respect. His world is beginning to change; his moral compass has lost its bearings and seems to waver.

After Valjean has dragged the wounded body of Marius through the sewers, he encounters the rogue Thénardier and, as he emerges into the night air of Paris, Javert is lurking. He lays his hands on Valjean. It seems that at last he has captured the escaped convict, and when asked if he will grant him a last request to return the near-dead Marius to his grandfather's house, at first he refuses and threatens to shoot Valjean if he takes another step. He cannot enforce the threat. Doubt has entered Javert's mind.

What is especially distressing to Javert is the way in which he cannot comprehend the generosity shown to him by Valjean when he allows him to escape from the barricades and doesn't kill him as ordered by the student insurgent. Suddenly Valjean and Monsieur Madelaine seem to merge into a figure that deserves veneration. For Javert, this amounts to admiration for a convicted felon; a man who returns good for evil. It isn't just the recognition that a convict *does* return good for evil, it is the understanding that such a thing could be possible at all in his black and white world that causes the distress. The inner turmoil that faces Javert is vocalised in the lyrics of the musical, but in Hugo's words as he goes to arrest Valjean, an inner voice restrained him: 'You will deliver up your deliverer? Then go and find Pilate's bowl and wash your hands.'

But his greatest anguish was the loss of certainty. He had been torn up by the roots. The code he lived by was in fragments in his hand. He was confronted by scruples that were utterly strange to him. He could no longer live by his lifelong principles; he had entered a new strange world of humanity, mercy, gratitude and justice other than that of the law ... He was forced to admit that kindness existed. The felon had been kind, and, a thing unheard of, so had he. Therefore he had failed himself. He felt himself to be a coward. Javert's ideal was to be more than human; to be above reproach. And he had failed.

All kinds of new questions arose in his mind, and the answers appalled him. Had the man performed a duty in showing him mercy? No, he had done something more. And he, in returning mercy, had denied his duty. So it seemed that there was something other than duty? Here all balance left him, the whole structure of his life collapsed; what was high was no more deserving of honour than what was low. Although instinctively he held the church in respect, he regarded it as no more than an august part of the social order; and order was his dogma, and had hitherto sufficed him. The police force had been his true religion. He had a superior officer, Monsieur Gisquet;[1] he had given no thought to that higher superior, which is God.[2]

And then he becomes conscious of God, and confused by this unexpected presence. In Javert's experience he has always treated a superior with respect and deference. He has always known that a subordinate should always give way and never dispute orders. If he cannot carry out his duties, he can resign. But how do we resign from God's authority?

To feel emotion was terrible. To be carved in stone, the very figure of chastisement, and to discover suddenly under the granite of our face something contradictory that is almost a heart ... He was forced to admit that infallibility is not always infallible, that there may be error in dogma, that society is not perfect, that a flaw in the unalterable is possible, that judges are men and even the law may do wrong. What was happening to Javert resembled the derailing of a train – the straight line of the soul broken by the presence of God. God, the inwardness of man, the true conscience as opposed to the false; the eternal, splendid presence. Did he understand or fully realize this? No ... He was not used to confronting the unknown. Until now what had been above him had been plain and simple, clearly defined and exact. Authority ... Javert had been conscious of nothing unknowable. The unexpected, the glimpse of chaos, these belonged to some unknown, recalcitrant, miserable world. But now, recoiling, he was appalled by a new manifestation – an abyss above him. It meant that he was wholly at a loss. In what was he to believe?[3]

These thoughts prompt provocative questions; was it possible that there are cases when the law is subject to transfigured crime? Does anarchy itself descend from heaven? For Javert to contemplate this was impossible, for it meant that all that seemed settled – the verdict of the court, the force of law, official wisdom, legal infallibility and the dogma that held society together – was lost.

Session Four

Duty to the law

Show: Watch the section showing the confrontation between Javert and Valjean following on from Fantine's death in the sanatorium, starting 'Valjean, at last' until Valjean's escape. *(2 mins)*

Alternatively, listen to or read the lyrics of 'The Confrontation'. *(2 mins)*

Discuss: Cardinal Newman is famous for saying, 'To live is to change, and to be perfect is to have changed often.' Javert believes that neither he nor Valjean can change. Think about change and how far it is possible. Is Javert right? *(3 mins)*

Ask: How does Valjean's sense of justice conflict with that of Javert? *(5 mins)*

The way of the Lord?

Show: Watch the scene from when Valjean and Cosette arrive at the north gate of Paris until to the end of Javert's solo set against the night sky of Paris. *(5 mins)*

Alternatively, listen to or read the lyrics of 'Stars'. *(3 mins)*

Discuss: We have already considered 'righteousness' when thinking about Fantine. What is Javert's understanding of righteousness? Look at Psalm 1 again. *(5 mins)*

Read:

> By the sweat of your face
> You shall eat bread
> Until you return to the ground,
> For out of it you were taken;
> You are dust,
> And to dust you shall return.

(Genesis 3:19) *(1 min)*

Discuss: This verse has become part of the Ash Wednesday liturgy for the imposition of ashes.

Does this verse encapsulate Javert's belief? Where does his understanding fall short?

How do we respond to Javert's sentiment that those who falter and fall should pay the price? *(5 mins)*

Reflect: Javert remains confident in his world-view until he is faced with the forgiveness of his adversary, and it is then that his world falls apart. *(2 mins)*

I am the law ...

Show: Watch the film from when Javert returns to the bloodied and deserted barricades until his death. *(6 mins)*

Alternatively, listen to or read the lyrics of 'Javert's Suicide'. *(3 mins)*

Reflect: The internal turmoil that Javert faces is similar to that experienced by Valjean when the bishop gives him the candlesticks and lets him go free. They are both responding to an act of compassion. Take a little time to reflect on the different ways they respond. *(3 mins)*

Discuss: Javert asks if the sins of Valjean can be forgiven. What do you think? *(3 mins)*

Reflect: Share stories informally of those you know or have read about who have lived 'bad' lives, that appear to have experienced truly life-transforming encounters with God. *(3 mins)*

Discuss: The majority of those who have seen the film or the stage musical probably believe that Valjean was not guilty of a crime. After all, as he states himself, he only stole a loaf of bread to feed a starving child. However, in the narrative, Hugo portrays Valjean as having a sense of sin, and he is also presented in the film in such a way. What are your thoughts? *(3 mins)*

Ask: We have reflected on original sin. Does this doctrine help us understand the nature of sin and what it means to be human? Can we explain this in a meaningful way to a non-Christian? *(5 mins)*

Read: Romans 3:21–26 *(1 min)*

Discuss: What would Javert make of it? There is always a tension between God's law, understood here as the Mosaic Law, and the law of the land. Is our moral conduct always governed by such rigid structures? *(3 mins)*

Read: Ezekiel 36:22–32 *(2 mins)*

Discuss: Just as Javert sees no alternative but to end his life, he sings that his heart is stone and yet it still trembles. Think again of the passages we have read about hearts of stone. Could Javert be saved or was he irredeemable? *(5 mins)*

Ask: Which character or group of people in the New Testament is closest to Javert? *(2 mins)*

Ask: Can we recognise similar types of people in society today? *(3 mins)*

Discuss: '… all have sinned and fall short of the glory of God' (Romans 3:23). We are 'dust' (Genesis 3:19). Can we accept that we all need God's grace, and that only God can help us change? *(3 mins)*

Reflect: Has this Lenten journey made you think about your own personal view of 'law' and 'grace'? Are you seeing the emptiness of 'rules' when presented with grace? Has this course challenged your understanding of the character of a God of grace who freely forgives? *(2 mins)*

Closing prayers

Heavenly Father, Almighty and everlasting God, grant us the discernment and wisdom to distinguish your will.
Help us to fulfil and exceed our duties to you and to those around us and not be governed by the emptiness of rules.
Help us to recognise and accept your loving-kindness and respond to the gift of grace.

We bring before you all those who feel unworthy and cannot contemplate change.
We pray for those charged with enforcing law and order; grant they may be true to themselves and compassionate in carrying out their duties.

We pray especially for those who are faced with uncertainty and doubt and for those for whom life begins to seem meaningless.

WEEK FIVE

Redemption and Salvation

In the beginning was the Word, and the Word was with God, and the Word was God. He was in the beginning with God. All things came into being through him, and without him not one thing came into being. What has come into being in him was life, and the life was the light of all people. The light shines in the darkness, and the darkness did not overcome it.
(John 1:1–5)

'The pupil dilates in darkness and in the end finds light, just as the soul dilates in misfortune and in the end finds God.'
(*Les Misérables*, Jean Valjean bears Marius through the sewers of Paris)[1]

Leaders' note

'Redemption' and 'salvation'… what do these words really mean? They are not just theological terms, but important truths. It may be good to introduce this theme informally before you begin; what do ideas of 'redemption' and 'salvation' mean for the group, individually?

The aim of this session is to bring together all the strands of the Lenten journey with *Les Misérables*; specifically, that the group might consider the true meaning of forgiveness, of a love that keeps no record of wrongs; of a turning away from darkness as we experience grace – and in that transformation, how we might bring hope to others.

Lent is a time of self-examination. As you come to the end of this course, make sure the group, while self-examining, look up to the coming of Easter; the pain of the cross, but after that, the resurrection and the promise of new life.

To start you thinking

The ideas of redemption and salvation are difficult to grasp, especially in the modern world, when there seems so much to be concerned about. These things look beyond this life, and yet at the same time they offer solace for this life. In the Gospels we get a sense of what theologians call 'realised eschatology'. Eschatology describes the end towards which this world and our own lives progress, and yet Jesus proclaims that the kingdom of God has already arrived; thus 'realised eschatology' is a way of trying to describe this. There is a difficult and obvious paradox about this notion. I remember leading a small Sunday school group some years ago and getting them to think about how God's kingdom could be around us, while at the same time there are so many dreadful things happening in the world. The children didn't seem to find this at all difficult. It was as if the love and security they felt and received from those around them existed in a different dimension from what is threatening about the world. Surely it was obvious that these things could coexist.

The other important aspect about eschatology is that it cannot be defined by humanity as a fixed goal with specific characteristics. The end of things and the ends of our lives and how they are measured may be known to God, but they cannot be known by us:

> For now we see in a mirror, dimly [or 'through a glass, darkly' (KJV) as my churchwarden would insist], but then we will see face to face. Now I know only in part; but then I will know fully, even as I have been fully known.
> (1 Corinthians 13:11,12)

This notion of uncertainty is crucial, because any journey of faith cannot be along fixed lines. It is not what modern politicians like to call a 'road map' and are then surprised and disappointed when the road doesn't do what it is supposed to do. Societies and faith groups that have a rigid sense of development and destination exclude the experience of the individual; indeed, they make personal reflection and examination impossible. This is a characteristic of fundamentalist belief and theologies; there is no room for the individual and what his or her unique encounter with God brings to humanity. Just as there needs to be an openness in the way we respond to a story such as *Les Misérables*, there needs to be an openness to the way we respond to God's presence in the Scriptures, in those around us and in our lives. There is no one-size-fits-all faith.

> We know that the whole creation has been groaning in labour pains until now; and not only the creation, but we ourselves, who have the first fruits of the Spirit, groan inwardly while we wait for adoption, the redemption of our bodies. For in hope we were saved. Now hope that is seen is not hope. For who hopes for what is seen? But if we hope

for what we do not see, we wait for it with patience.
(Romans 8:22–25)

As we have seen, Javert's tragedy was that he lived in a fixed
universe that does not allow for change. He could not face
the possibility that wrongs could be forgiven. Worse than
that, he could not face the possibility that the structures of
society and the law could be flawed in any way. If our hope
is something fixed and clearly defined, there is nothing for
us to engage with; there is no challenge; eventually we are
trapped in a mechanistic universe, like Javert. Very recently
the European Court gave judgement on the cases of Jeremy
Bamber, Peter Moore and Douglas Vinter, ruling that not
allowing the possibility of a review for parole is an abrogation
of a basic human right – the right to hope. It could be argued
that it is hard to see why those who have committed brutal,
unprovoked murders should be allowed to seek a review of
their case at the expense of the taxpayer. Have they not denied
the basic right of human life to another soul? Yet it seems
that the judgement wasn't about a right to freedom, but that it
should never be completely ruled out. There is nothing in the
judgement that compels the authorities to release any of these
men in future, just that it should be a possibility, however
faint. Javert had lost the gift of hope.

Hugo's novel and the musical version are both about
hope. Hugo prefaced the novel in 1862 with words written
at his home in Guernsey, where he lived after being exiled by
Napoleon III for his disapproval of the new regime:

While through the working of laws and customs there
continues to exist a condition of social condemnation
which artificially creates a human hell within civilization,
and complicates with human fatality a destiny that is
divine; while the three great problems of this century,
the degradation of man in the proletariat, the subjection
of women through hunger, the atrophy of the child by
darkness, continue unresolved; while in some regions

social asphyxia remains possible; in other words, and in
still wider terms, while ignorance and poverty persist on
earth, books such as this cannot fail to be of value.[2]

For Hugo, there was an important political imperative that
society's wrongs should be recognised and put right. His work
is set against the troubled history of France in the first half of
the nineteenth century and he is clearly passionate about social
justice. The backdrop to the confrontation between Valjean
and Javert is the tragedy of the people. They are striving for
the light. Isaiah promises a return for the exiles. The people
of God are to be brought home but they, too, must be purged.
They must receive a new heart. This hope is not just a vague,
general feeling that everything is going to be all right; it is
a profound hope that things will be changed by individuals
working and bound together by love. Hugo tells us a story
of how people can transform the world, and however little
they may seem to achieve, they can be transformed by their
sacrifice and their efforts.

The musical and film versions, too, cannot but fail to stir us
as we see young men fighting for the people. There is a sense
of the romantic; self-sacrifice for the greater good. Gavroche,
a symbol of the downtrodden and defenceless in society,
is brutally slaughtered. But although society is in need of
salvation, so too is the individual.

For Marius and Cosette, the reward is to find love in this
life. They find the joy and thrill of physical and human love,
and they will be transformed by it. There is a little incident
in the novel where Marius, having discovered at last where
Cosette lives, leaves a notebook under a stone in the garden
at the back of the house in *rue Plumet*. It is a string of lovers'
thoughts that place God at the heart of any form of love.

The first epistle of John reminds that love is of God (1 John
4:7). Physical love, the love between a man and a woman, can
also help lead us to God. Valjean understands that he must
relinquish his paternal love for Cosette in order for her to be
released and grow. But it is Valjean who is the principal soul,

whose life unfolds and is transformed. The bishop sees that the revolutionary had acted for good to try to bring about change; through his encounter, he understands that the spiritual life cannot be divorced from a life that seeks to change and bring good to the world, however difficult the moral choices may be and however much suffering that may entail.

Valjean's life is transformed spiritually by an act of grace, but he still has to live out the implications of it. To fully receive grace is to be changed by it. It is not enough to feel the presence of God. In a short section, Hugo writes against daydreamers; those who think but don't act. I must confess that from time to time I am guilty of sitting with a glass of wine on a summer's evening and reflecting on the wonders of nature around me and what is good about the world, as well as what is wrong; as if that were enough. Valjean responds by creating wealth for himself and for others, by giving himself up for an honest man, by nurturing Cosette to satisfy her mother's wishes, by saving Marius, by little acts of kindness, by allowing Cosette to love and, last of all, by seeking to disappear lest his identity brings ruin on Cosette.

Victor Hugo had some very forward-looking and progressive political ideas, but his theology was remarkably conservative. He thought of himself as a free thinker later in life, but he began as a Roman Catholic. His free thinking is evident in the way he describes God, his conservatism in the orthodox view that a price must be paid for the lost to be redeemed. Thus Fantine pays for her mistakes and loses her life that Cosette may flourish. Valjean's sin, too, although to modern eyes inconsequential, is a burden he is aware of and a burden that he suffers for. There is great power in the moral choice he has to face when he struggles with his conscience as to whether he should reveal his true identity and save the innocent man held in his place. He knows that if he speaks, he is condemned, and if he stays silent, he is damned. Grace is symbolised by the silver candlesticks that he keeps to remind him of the bishop's kindness. Through this act of kindness he gains wealth and status, and yet he has to sacrifice it. Through his self-sacrifice in giving himself up, he is rewarded with the gift of love, forged in his need to protect and nurture Cosette, and yet again he has to relinquish it so that Cosette's own love and life may blossom. He is redeemed by responding to the gift of grace.

It was the compassion of the bishop coupled with his words that challenged Valjean to seek a new path. And at the end of the film, he prays, 'Bring me home.'

Hugo ends his great work with two paragraphs that were omitted from the first published version of his book.

> Nevertheless, those who study the health of society must now and then shake their heads. Even the strongest-minded and most clear thinking must have their moments of misgiving. Will the future ever arrive? The question seems almost justified when one considers the shadows looming ahead, the sombre confrontation of egoists and outcasts. On the side of the egoists, prejudice – that darkness of a rich education – appetite that grows with intoxication, the bemusement of prosperity which blunts the sense, the fear of suffering which in some cases goes so far as to hate all sufferers, and unshakeable complacency, the ego so inflated that it stifles the soul; and on the side of the outcasts, greed and envy, resentment at the happiness of others, the turmoil of the human animal in search of personal fulfilment, hearts filled with fog, misery, needs, and fatalism, and simple, impure ignorance.
>
> Should we continue to look upwards? Is the light we can see in the sky one of those which will presently be extinguished? The ideal is terrifying to behold, lost as it is in the depths, small, isolated, a pin-point, brilliant but threatened on all sides by the dark forces that surround it: nevertheless, no more in danger than a star in the jaws of the clouds.[3]

The first paragraph could have been written very recently, commenting on Western society today, and is remarkable for that alone. I have often returned to the second to gain a sense of hope in adversity. The gift of hope itself is an outpouring of grace.

Session Five

Bring us home

Show: Watch the scene on the barricades just after Valjean fires a false shot to make the others think he has killed Javert. *(4 mins)*

Alternatively, listen to or read the lyrics of 'Bring Him Home'. *(4 mins)*

Reflect: This powerful lyric is a prayer for Marius but also an acknowledgement that Valjean himself must release Cosette. As we have seen, Valjean prays to God to bring him home. There are echoes of 'homecoming' in several different parts of the film. There is another reference which might easily be missed. As Marius's grandfather, Monsieur Gillenormand, comes down the stairs when Valjean, Cosette and Marius arrive, the main lyric is a heart full of love, but he sings one short sentence about his grandson being home. He has longed for the return of Marius and that he comes with his heart full of love is another metaphor for a homecoming in a spirit of reconciliation and forgiveness. *(4 mins)*

Read: The best known biblical text for homecoming must be the Parable of the Prodigal Son. Take a few moments to read Luke 15:11–32. *(3 mins)*

Ask: The picture in the song is different from the parable. Do you find any similarities? *(3 mins)*

Ask: Can we imagine the father in the parable having similar thoughts to those expressed in the song? *(4 mins)*

Reflect: Take a moment to reflect on the words of the liturgy for Holy Communion, '… when we were still far off you met us in your Son and brought us home.' *(4 mins)*

Who am I?

Reflect: 'Who am I?' is a short interrogatory statement that recurs in several of the lyrics in *Les Misérables*. It is the statement Valjean makes in the courtroom in Arras when he gives himself up, and it is the question he asks Marius before he decides to hide his identity from Cosette. Significantly, Javert doesn't ask himself the question; he simply asks, 'Who is this man?' about Valjean, when he fails to comprehend why he doesn't take revenge. *(5 mins)*

Show: Watch the scene from when they arrive at Monsieur Gillenormand's home, after the number 'Empty Chairs and Tables', 'A Heart Full of Love' until the end, 'You're Jean Valjean'. *(3½ mins)*

Alternatively, listen to or read the lyrics of 'Valjean's Confession'. *(3 mins)*

Reflect: There is an excellent film called *Beyond Right and Wrong*,[4] which examines several places of deep conflict in the world. It covers the situation in Palestine, the disastrous racial slaughter and killing in Rwanda, and the conflict in Northern Ireland. It is a series of moving encounters with those who lost loved ones, and in many cases the victim and the perpetrators meet each other. Clearly it takes enormous courage on both sides. The most powerful encounter for me was that between Jo Berry and Patrick Magee.

Jo Berry was the daughter of Sir Anthony Berry, one of those killed by the IRA when the Grand Hotel in Brighton was bombed during the Conservative Party Conference. Patrick Magee was one of those convicted of the bombing.

He served ten years in prison before he was released under the Good Friday Agreement. In an attempt to deal with the grief of losing her father, Jo Berry had made contact with the IRA soon after the bombing, but she had not met Paddy Magee while he was in prison. After he was released, she organised a meeting.

At the screening of the film that I witnessed, both Paddy Magee and Jo Berry were present in person and answered questions afterwards. They sat next to each other, and it would be fair to say that they have become friends. They travel to different troubled parts of the world to share their experiences. They both described their first meeting in Dublin. Magee said that at first he had just talked about the armed struggle, how and why he believed in it and why he had involved himself in terrorist acts; as he talked on, he described how he realised that Jo Berry was not an ideology, not an embodiment of British Imperialism, but simply another person. As he stopped speaking to her, he said suddenly he didn't know who he was. *(5 mins)*

Ask: What does Jean Valjean mean when he cries out, 'Who am I?' Is he simply posing a question to be taken literally? *(3 mins)*

Ask: How has he questioned his identity since the bishop gave him the candlesticks? *(3 mins)*

Ask: Do we need to ask who we are before another story can begin? *(5 mins)*

Show: Watch the final section of the musical from when Marius and Cosette arrive at the convent to the end. *(6 mins)*
Alternatively, listen to or read the lyrics of 'The Epilogue'. *(6 mins)*

Reflect: This final number interweaving the voices of the principals and the stirring chorus is brimful of images and

biblical resonances. An obvious passage is Micah 4:1–4.
Think about other passages that spring to mind. *(5 mins)*

Discuss: Valjean prays for grace to be shown to Marius and
Cosette. How does the grace of God transform the characters
of *Les Misérables*? Did another story begin? *(5 mins)*

Reflect: Do the sufferings of Valjean, Fantine and others lead
them to redemption and salvation? In the context of Jesus'
death on the cross, ask yourself how are they changed. *(3 mins)*

Ask: As we move towards Easter, can another story begin –
for us, and for those around us? *(3 mins)*

Discuss: How? *(5 mins)*

Closing prayers

*Heavenly Father, Almighty and everlasting God, we thank you
for our time together this Lent. We pray that we may have
been moved by reflecting on the story of Jean Valjean.
Give us grace to examine our own lives.
Give us grace to show and manifest the love you have shown
    to us in the life of your Son, Jesus Christ.*

*Bring home all those who are 'far off'; grant that as you meet
    us you may reach out and meet them.
Bring home all those who are divided from your love.*

*Grant that we may truly see your face in those around us.
Grant that those who hate may be turned to love, that we will
    live again in freedom in the garden of the Lord.*

*Grant us redemption and salvation through your heavenly
    grace. Amen.*

Further Thoughts

The novel, the film and the stage version of *Les Misérables* raise so many questions about faith, God and Christianity that it would be impossible to cover them all in a short course which tries to stick the main themes of the season of Lent. I have made some suggestions and short notes on other topics or sections of the film that might be discussed. This could take place in an organised way, in groups, or privately.

1. THE BISHOP
'Conscience is the amount of inner knowledge we possess.' These words of Monsieur G are a perceptive comment on how we view ourselves. It is so easy to overlook aspects of our characters, just as the bishop assumes he has the moral high ground when he visits the recluse.

The bishop has made the mistake of imagining that Monsieur G should have lived life according to his rules, and of failing to see that he lived life in the way that he thought best under the circumstances. He admits that he tore up the altar clothes, but that it was to bind the wound of the country.

Discuss: How far as a society and as individuals do we heed and follow the teaching of Matthew 5:38–46?

2. VALJEAN
Although we do not condemn people to hard labour for stealing a crust of bread, it could be said that we still imprison people for crimes when they might be dealt with in a different way.

Discuss: Are there lessons for how we administer criminal justice in Valjean's experience?

3. JAVERT

There is so much that is fascinating about Javert. In spite of the fact that we know him to be wrong, we can identify with much of his thinking. On the question of how society deals with criminals, for example, there is a lot in his thinking that would be supported by large numbers of people today. As I mentioned in the section on Valjean, around 45 per cent of the prison population that I came across had chosen crime as a career path. Showing them clemency and mercy would do nothing to bring them round to a different way of life. In many cases, they simply cannot make what they would consider a worthwhile living in any other way. It is not helpful releasing repeat offenders. But Javert treats everyone who has transgressed as irredeemable and forever tainted with sin. Ezekiel deals with exactly this problem in chapter 18. Verses 26–29 encapsulate this very question:

> When the righteous turn away from their righteousness and commit iniquity, they shall die for it; for the iniquity that they have committed they shall die. Again, when the wicked turn away from the wickedness they have committed and do what is lawful and right, they shall save their life. Because they considered and turned away from all the transgressions that they had committed, they shall surely live; they shall not die. Yet the house of Israel says, 'The way of the Lord is unfair.' O House of Israel, are my ways unfair? Is it not your ways that are unfair?

There is a genuine dilemma here. It is the tension between mercy and justice. On one occasion, I picked up a hitchhiker who gave me a story about having lost his wallet and not having any cash. He described in a matter of fact way that he couldn't make it to his next destination and could I let him have £30, which he would return to me? There were quite a number of elements that seemed plausible, and they may well have been, so I gave him the cash and my address. I didn't hear any more. So who was the idiot? Him or me?

There are lots of interesting questions about Javert's approach to the law that are worthy of reflection, but the other point that most springs out at me is the way in which Javert cannot handle any suggestion of doubt. His belief in the law and the structures of society are so inflexible that the idea they might be flawed in the slightest way is something he cannot bear to contemplate; in the end it pushes him over the edge.

In the last fifty years or so we have seen a huge change in attitudes to the authority of the church, or any moral authority, for that matter. I come across many people who want their parish priest, their bishops and most of all the Archbishop of Canterbury, to tell them what to think. They want the moral certainties to be decided by someone else. They feel there are so many things that the church doesn't take a strong line on these days, when it should give firm moral instruction. This is just how Javert feels.

There are lots of complex reasons for the shift, and of course some conservative congregations do take a very strong line on many issues. One reason is the reduction in numbers within the parishes, meaning that the laity needs to be prepared to take a greater responsibility. But in the end it is the individual who needs to engage properly with moral issues and what they mean for each of us. This is something Javert cannot do.

Discuss: Where do you look for moral certainties? What are some of the moral issues you are faced with in your family, at work, with neighbours and friends? How far do people look to *you* for moral certainties? How do you feel about that?

End Notes

INTRODUCTION
1. Victor Hugo, *Les Misérables*, translation by Norman Denny (London: Penguin Books, 1980), p.110. First published by The Folio Society, 1976.
2. Ibid., p.111.
3. Rowan Williams, *Dostoevsky: Language, Faith and Fiction* (London: Continuum, 2010), p.60.

WEEK ONE
1. Hugo, *Les Misérables*, p.1229.

WEEK TWO
1. Hugo, *Les Misérables*, p.25.
2. Ibid., p.52.
3. Cartouche was an infamous bandit and highwayman executed on the wheel in 1721; much more shockingly his young brother was hung with a rope under his armpits on 31 July 1722 on no evidence of wrongdoing at all. He begged to be put out of pain but after two hours he was taken down and found to be dead.
4. Hugo, *Les Misérables*, p.54.
5. Ibid., p.57.
6. Keith Jones, *Adam's Dream: Human Longings and the Love of God* (London: Mowbray, 2007), p. 102.

WEEK THREE

1. It is also worth noting that at the time there was a high level of suicide amongst the young offenders. This was not on account of being locked up, but often because they were fearful about being released into a community where there was no structure to their lives and they were at the mercy of drug dealers and other gang leaders.
2. Hugo, *Les Misérables*, p.115.
3. Ibid., p.159.
4. Ibid., p.159.
5. Ibid., p.212.
6. Ibid., p.257.

WEEK FOUR

1. Henri Gisquet was a real character appointed chief of police in 1831 and noted for his brutal suppression of the 1832 insurrection. He ordered all doctors and surgeons to report any wounded to the police after the rising. Hugo comments on this, noting that most refused to comply with his command, which is why Marius was not reported as he convalesced.
2. Hugo, *Les Misérables*, p.1106.
3. Ibid., p.1107.

WEEK FIVE

1. Hugo, *Les Misérables*, p.1078.
2. Ibid., p.15.
3. Ibid., p.1232.
4. As I reflected again on this film and how it resonates with Valjean's cry of 'Who am I?', I noticed among published responses to this encounter on the website www. theforgivenessproject.com, the following:

This site cracked open my heart, and made me look at the world in general and my life in particular in a new way.

Brace yourself. It may haunt you. The issue addressed here
– forgiveness – could save our world. I am rarely as moved
by a single site as I was by this one.

In view of the biblical references to the hardness of heart
that we so often feel, I was particularly struck by the
comment. As well as this response, Jo Berry is published as
saying, 'I'm beginning to realise that no matter which side
of the conflict you're on, had we all lived each other's lives,
we could all have done what the other did.' Surely this is
the kind of self-knowledge that the bishop gained when he
encountered Monsieur G.